Making a Salad:

Wedge vs. Inclined Plane

by Mari Schuh

Lerner Publications ◆ Minneapolis

LERNER

SOURCE™

Expand learning beyond the printed book. Download free, complementary educational resources for this book from our website, www.lerneresource.com.

All images in this book are used with the permission of: © Todd Strand/Independent Picture Service except: © Fotokostic/Shutterstock.com, p. 9; © Louella938/Shutterstock.com, p. 14 (middle left); © iStockphoto.com/sandyriverman, p. 14 (bottom); © Shariff Che\' Lah/Dreamstime.com, p. 14 (top); © T photography/Shutterstock.com, p. 15; © iStockphoto.com/DusanBartolovic, p. 16; © iStockphoto.com/kali9, p. 17; © iStockphoto.com/SergioZacchi, p. 18.

Front cover: © Todd Strand/Independent Picture Service.

Main body text set in ITC Avant Garde Gothic Std Medium 21/25.
Typeface provided by Adobe Systems.

Lerner Publications Company
A division of Lerner Publishing Group, Inc.
241 First Avenue North
Minneapolis, MN 55401 USA

For reading levels and more information, look up this title at www.lernerbooks.com.

Library of Congress Cataloging-in-Publication Data

Schuh, Mari C., 1975- author.
    Making a salad : wedge vs. inclined plane / by Mari Schuh.
        pages cm — (First step nonfiction. Simple machines to the rescue)
    Audience: 5–8.
    Audience: K to 3.
        ISBN 978-1-4677-8028-5 (lb : alk. paper) — ISBN 978-1-4677-8294-4 (pb : alk. paper) — ISBN 978-1-4677-8295-1 (eb pdf)
        1. Wedges—Juvenile literature. 2. Inclined planes—Juvenile literature. 3. Simple machines—Juvenile literature. I. Title. II. Series: First step nonfiction. Simple machines to the rescue.
TJ147.S4187 2016
621.8—dc23   2015001944

Manufactured in the United States of America
1 – CG – 7/15/15

Table of Contents

Helping in the Kitchen

Liz and her dad are making dinner.

Liz washes lettuce.

She wants to make a salad.

Liz's dad slices tomatoes.
He uses a knife.

Wedges push objects apart.

The knife is a **wedge**. A wedge is a **simple machine**.

8

This wedge pushes an egg away from a pan.

Wedges can lift objects.

Liz's dad wants to add the tomatoes to the salad.

He tries to lift the tomatoes with the knife.

The knife is sharp. Liz doesn't want her dad to get hurt.

Liz has an idea! She lifts
one end of the cutting
board.

These are examples of simple machines.

The board is an **inclined plane**. An inclined plane is a simple machine.

The street helps the streetcar go down.

Inclined planes can help objects move up or down.

An inclined plane has a
slanted surface.

These people use force to move boxes up a ramp.

Force helps objects move up an inclined plane.

17

Gravity pulls this boy down the slide.

Gravity pulls objects down an inclined plane.

Liz thinks gravity can help move the tomatoes.

Time to Eat!

Liz lifts the cutting board.
The tomatoes fall into the
20 bowl.

The inclined plane helped
Liz and her dad!

How can an inclined plane help you?

Now it's time for dinner!

Glossary

force – pushing and pulling on an object

gravity – the pull of Earth that makes things fall to the ground

inclined plane – a flat, slanted surface

simple machine – a machine with one moving part or no moving parts

wedge – a machine that pushes objects apart or holds them together

Index